"John Dorsey's book is a tribute to small town life. He carefully dissects the lives of his characters to find the crossroads where dreams were thwarted, and how the survivors of these lost dreams manage to carry on anyway, sometimes as though they don't even know how close they came to escaping the bear trap of smoky bars and bar fights and the endless cycle of pregnancy and childrearing. Each inhabitant of these poems is treated with delicate dignity, leaving you with the feeling that you've met each and every one of these characters at some point in your own life, or may have even been in one of two of these poems yourself."

-Holly Day, author of *Into The Cracks*

"John Dorsey is one of my favorite living poets - clear minute particulars and broken-hearted honesty. Generous empathetic outlook for our hardened times."

-Marc Olmsted, author of *Don't Hesitate: Knowing Allen Ginsberg*

"There's a bleakness to the landscape of John Dorsey's characters. The clouds are always low. Someone is always scraping together money for a cheeseburger or a pint of wine. Despite that, the landscape is livable because the cheeseburgers are tasty and the wine quenches a thirst. His characters know that "painting flowers with a closed fist / lacks imagination." Reading this fine collection is like coming upon a magical "tar paper shack / full of poems / & beehives / & music."

-Mike James, author of *Leftover Distances*

SUNDOWN AT THE REDNECK CARNIVAL

Poems by John Dorsey

Spartan Press

Spartan Press

Kansas City, MO

spartanpress.com

Spartan
Press

Copyright © John Dorsey, 2022

First Edition: 1 3 5 7 9 10 8 6 4 2

ISBN: 978-1-952411-93-9

LCCN: 2022930012

Author photo: John Burroughs

Acknowledgments:

Thanks is given to the staff & board of Osage Arts
Community, where this work was created.

Work included has appeared in or is forthcoming in *San
Pedro River Review, Trampoline, The Coop, Live Nude Poems,
Roadside Raven Review, Lothlorien Poetry Journal, Rusty
Truck Zine, Fixator Press* and *GAS Poetry and Art* —
Grateful acknowledgement is given to the publishers..

Table of Contents

Sundown at the Redneck Carnival are sacred songs from a trailer park hymnal for the dead, a macrocosm of red, white and blues America. A well-loved album of family photos, snapshots of forgiveness. A thanksgiving for the disenfranchised, big game hunting with the ghosts of spreading ink. John is old school in that he is dedicated to his craft and writes what he knows, what he lives, no differently than Charles Bukowski celebrated the arguing drunks on the other side of the thin walls of a skid row flop on the nickel or the win, place or show of the track. Through his observations John becomes a familiar, a literary vessel for those that he encounters in his day to day doing what it is that the best of any creative talent might accomplish; he embraces the ordinary and elevates it to an extraordinary level in such an ordinary way that anyone might receive it. Like Charles Bukowski, John Sweet or Justin Hyde, John celebrates the commonplace taking that which is taken for granted by most anyone and transforming it into something not better than it was, but as good as it is. He divines the dim magic out of the stale hustle of a pool room, imbues a cheap plastic promise ring with the hard beauty of a sparkling diamond and casts an abandoned teenage mother with a baby under arm each arm as a lost and lonely Venus in a love story held together with tape.

And so, as the sun sets on the once upon a time of the American west, as voting rights languish in the purgatory of Congress, as the unmasked go selfishly masked behind the ignorant courage of their toxic convictions into the repeat and change viral dance-a-thon of Covid über alles, as the Supreme Court feigns impartiality hearing arguments from Mississippi (Goddamn!), as John Dorsey considers the prettiest girl in town pregnant for the third time in three years, we bid farewell to any reason embracing the present fiction that sets fire to all that we think we know as we trip not so gently into that carnival Missouri night with John, the poem, and a reasonable voice that can find you, if you listen.

S.A. Griffin
Los Angeles, CA
December 4, 2021

for Mark & Tony, with gratitude for their support.

SUNDOWN AT THE REDNECK CARNIVAL

Sundown at the Redneck Carnival

gordon lightfoot plays on the jukebox
as a dozen guys in flannel
test their strength
while pounding light beer
by the pitcher
as a young boy with a mullet
wanders the room
looking as lost as he'll ever be
the ghost of his own future
a smudge of dirt on his cheek
or maybe it's printer's ink
the lindbergh baby left to rot
without the ransom note
neglect is a tattoo
he will never
be able to wash off

the prettiest girl in town
is pregnant for the third time
in three years

the way she sways
her hips
is an omen

she pours drinks
& becomes a wingless canary

singing for tips
in a cage filled with stale smoke

the song says you'd better beware
as the claw machine drops a stuffed teddy bear
with a bright red tongue

but gordon lightfoot might as well
be talking to the dead

nobody listens for warnings here

as the boy dreams
of his father
long gone

he imagines he's a grizzly
with a silent tongue
& bright red fists
who would never
raise a hand in anger

who's only there
to wipe his face
clean.

Poem for the Mothers

some of you dead
some hit by buses
on urgent street corners
some with skin as yellow
as a dying tulip
some with stomachs still growing
in a race with history
glowing with beauty
as the leaves blow with abandon
as each step leads you
further from the past

& somehow you've gotten younger
& i've aged a thousand years
just standing here
in front of the tree
outside your house
as the leaves blow loud
like invisible trumpets
with their rat a tat tat
on the siding
of every heart

a faded tattoo
carved into every
tree lined street

every memory
was once bright
before it became
a dying star.

Poem for Ida in 1986

gyrating shuttles like dandelions
their screams blowing away in the wind
mashed potatoes from an ice cream scoop
ice cream from an ice cream scoop
sweaty hands
no metal detectors
no bomb threats
the captain of the football team
stayed in the closet
& died inside

everyone was lonely

the occasional fist fight
solved everything & nothing
that went unsaid.

At the Neon, Winter 2004

snow falling the color of rust
in the bed
of a pickup
in dayton ohio

what happens in a taco bell drive thru
should stay there

like an old movie
there should be dancing
& less horns blaring
like we just won a war

the sky lit up
music swelling in the air
so crisp that a lover might dwell
on the leaving
as much as those precious first steps
moving forward
without knowing
what might happen next.

In the Morning

for Dan Wright & Carl Sandburg

maybe you would've liked each other
watching the fog creep in
each paw with its own shape
each body is a different city you could love
a gentle rain you could hold onto
or let slip away
through a crack
in the window
like an act
of forgiveness.

Inflation of the Covid Dead

in line at the register
a kid with buck teeth
& an old woman in a hoveround
wear matching faded t-shirts
for the local girl's volleyball team
like something out of a movie
that nobody would ever pay to see

they yell about the price of groceries

it's the president's fault
it's the news media

& don't you know
everyone's on meth

& the ghosts of the covid dead
aren't around to buy green beans
by the barrel
as if they had tulip fever

their faces turned blue
from coughing
trying to reason
with death in a past life
while holding their breath
in a paper mask.

East Coast/West Coast, in Southern Missouri

a high school girl with thick black glasses
& a baby bump barely concealed
by a second hand tupac t-shirt
stands on the front of her lawn
as a volunteer fireman
who didn't make it past the 9th grade
throws candy in her direction
with a pitching arm
that will never take him any further
than the next county over

a love story held together with tape
like the glasses
peeling in the summer sun

candy corn at her feet
like stray bullets
in a gang war
in a music video
that will last
the rest of her life

a baby under each arm
pacing east and west
a drive by that goes in circles
leading nowhere

always in a rivalry
with possibility

maybe the old owner of the shirt
fed the hungry
danced in an empty swimming pool
& swore there was music
that nobody else could hear

or maybe she actually saw
who killed tupac
& biggie both
& never said a word
because there was peace
in just letting things go
like the boy
who placed the shirt
over her shoulders
as she shivered
taking what she hadn't offered
to begin with

because when you wash out
the blood stains
all you're left with is
your own heartbreak

standing on your front lawn
wearing someone else's dream
shrunken down so many times

with wrinkles
that you can never
quite smooth out
until you're almost invisible
with a snow cone melting
down your arm
in the sun
bleeding red white & blue
as a single sock
fresh out of the dryer
sticks to your belly
& that's the best part
of your day.

Poem For Any Girl Who's Still Listening

my heart has always been
a tar paper shack
full of poems
& beehives
& music

come inside
& we will wait
for the wind
to catch up
together.

Poem for a Noseless Man

for victor clevenger

an old man with half his nose
eaten away by cancer
says we are all ravenous locusts
at the same overcrowded trough
as he explains his theories on women
the front half of his yellow sports car
torn off to match his nose
after swerving to miss a hay baler
he pumps gas and laughs
thinking about when he left home
after a fight with his father
& how he has been
on the road
ever since

he points to the car
it could have been worse
he could've ended up
like james dean

but he's not pretty enough for heaven
or the silver screen
& not ugly enough
to hide his face
& let some lonesome dirt road
forget he was ever here.

1987

a silver fiero catches fire
in the elementary school parking lot

oliver north practices the art of scat
on a black & white tv.

1995

wolfgang & i burn a joint in the woods
behind his grandfather's house

like stoned vampires who haven't slept in ages
we laugh as his girlfriend falls
into a dry creek bed
while attempting to walk
across a log
in jelly shoes.

For Tessa Lowell, Snapping Green Beans

letters between jim and e.e. cummings
hidden behind the cellar steps
become our theater for the afternoon

the young boys then looking for a father figure
in revolutionary times that just seemed ordinary
like the smell of burning tires
& crumbling hearts
that just gets lost in the weeds
along the cuyahoga river

those boys nearing seventy now
coming to help you in your garden
snapping green beans
moving memories around in the dirt
like pieces of heavy furniture
that you thought
you had gotten rid of.

Poem for my Grandmother, Dead at 61

i never remember you looking young
shaky hands lighting one cigarette
off the other
black rings under your eyes
but your smile was magic
talking about the tv preachers
by their first names
as if they really did care
about your salvation
as if they were going
to rescue you from your life
whenever the spirit moved them.

Renegades, 1989

all day i had badgered my mother
for $2.50 she barely had
i can hardly even remember the movie now
falling asleep halfway through

my chair squeaked
the rubber soles of my shoes
stuck to the floor

they had raised the price of candy
at the concession stand
earlier that day

god i wish
i had a time machine
to go back there.

Kris Buys His Girlfriend $200 Worth of Cheap Jewelry

in a mall that has since been torn down
& hours later
she breaks up with him
over his pager

making out with a guy
in the bathroom
next to the spencer's gifts

a promise ring for $5.99
thrown into a fountain
filled with loose change
& failed relationships
that started out as wishes
made in good faith.

Poem for Shelly Andrews

you had a big nose
i had a small dick

it was perfect.

Electra Glide in Blue with David Smith

none of us are out
on that highway alone
love is the only true thing there is
words kicking up dust
in the search for myth
we were in this together
that's what you never understood

for a moment
you held a dream
that felt real.

Young Man

david
i'm not saying
you were no good
just rotten on the inside
like a bag of sour apples
who left us too young.

Roanoke, Virginia, 1992

it was so warm
you could almost go shirtless
even at midnight
on the mini golf course
next to our hotel

my grandfather with his arm
around my shoulder
sweating through his windbreaker
he'd worn all the way from canada
looking out at the night sky
having perhaps his last clear vision
of an empty parking lot
before they switched off the lights
everything blurred after that
on prosthetic limbs
the little things
you can't ever get back
when you're no longer able
to run away
from the past.

Niagara Falls Haiku

undercooked eggs
walt whitman under newspapers
on a snow covered bench.

Trailer Park Song, 1996

for amber

a young girl making men out of boys
& boys out of old men
for 50 bucks a pop
hoping for a few more minutes
of puppy love
in an abandoned trailer

straddling the past
on a shag carpet
with cigarette burns
up & down
her arms.

Trailer Park Song, 1999

maybe there are still christmas lights
on the last night of a tired century
my cousin samantha still too young
to know about the future
riding on my back
as if i'm a horse
in a race with time
that none of us ever win

pockets empty
i search the tv screen
for a red haired girl
dancing under the stars
but nothing feels limitless
tonight.

Poem for My Mother

two fathers
neither of them any good
one mother dead
with four small children
at an age when most millennials
are still using youth
as an excuse
for everything
left unsaid
& the other held back
from a wider world
that would've loved her
with a cigarette burning
going no further
than the front yard.

A Funeral in Buffalo

for nathael stolte

the first time we met
we gorged ourselves
on $5 chinese food
down the street
from the bus station
& i waited in a parked car
while you went to a funeral
for an old high school friend
from your squatter days
who had overdosed
on sickness

& later that night
a dark haired girl
held your hand
sitting in some mobbed up dive
with shitty chicken fingers
where for a few moments
you seemed forever young.

Matthew Haines & the House Special

one jug of cheap red wine
somehow improves your driving
a young girl twists her hair with her finger
as she attempts to take our order
sliding into the booth to talk to you
& losing her job
by the time the local diner
closes for the night

maybe she needed her tips
to help her mother
keep the lights on
maybe she has a younger brother
or sister to feed
either way her high school sweater
& the glitter on her fingernails seems fresh
at an age where everything
feels uncertain
you reach for her phone
inserting your number
& your intentions
are clear.

Road Rage

a bee swirls through the car
& out the window
never once coming close
to your face
& i wish i could go with it
buzzing wild & free
as we hit a dying cedar tree
its skin covered with scars
by careless drivers
looking to sting anything
that can't move fast enough
to get out
of the way.

Painting Flowers with a Closed Fist or The Violent Femmes Are Not a Feminist Group

for becky hernandez

this is not a revolution
you were meant to remember
the words to

overhead the sun looks like a blister
in western pennsylvania in 1985

painting flowers with a closed fist
lacks imagination
& it is no way
to learn
how to dance.

Love Letters for Jana Horn

the mailbox is full of postcards
from hipster boys
& aging dreamers
who just want
to be swallowed whole
by a desert rose.

Trailer Park Song, 1982

my brother
angry
red faced
screaming
& beautiful.

Trailer Park Song, 1992

mary ann hums phil collins
into our rotary phone
it's a love song
even though it isn't
making me reach
for a kitchen knife
holding it close
as i hang up
& wait for the receiver
to go dead
before i go outside
to wait for my ride
to the movies.

Bob Creeley was an Asshole

for jake marx

that ungrateful chicken farmer
pecking away at your driving
as you wheeled him around the kent state campus
as tear gas and history
flew through glass windows
& he barked out orders
to go this way or that
the same year irving layton
sang leonard cohen
with the voice of a canary
with love & quiet dignity.

A Sea Shanty for Uncle Shippie

glam rock paul
never without a bottle
of vodka
halfway to fifty
at the edge of the millenium
dave graham shooting bad luck
through a needle
roman puking wormwood
into the bushes
off naudain street
jeff with a voice like a mouse
who never left brooklyn
candace looking on
beautiful & baked
wags missing in action
on a street corner
reserved for ghosts
shippie gone
drifting
into the waves
of the past.

Poem for Shelby

too young to remember jonbenet
it doesn't seem creepy to you
to ask for donations
for a baby beauty pageant

$10 here
$5 there
for a twirl
at the baton
of immortality

sometimes there
is nothing uglier
than
hope.

For Rusty, in a Pandemic Full of Justifications

a paper mask
can hardly keep out the smell
of old men & smoke
i miss it too
coughing out a siren's song
getting used to freedom
darts & george thorogood
for a few quarters
at the tips
of your fingers

pick any song you like
but nothing
can hold in fear.

Harvey Weinstein, Harvey Weinstein, Harvey Weinstein

your paws like a bear's
where you decided to place your hands
changed everything

because of you
i can't even tell a woman
that holding her hand
could change the whole trajectory
of my heart
without fear
on both sides

but the truth is
you aren't some disease
but merely a symptom
of something larger
than a pair of misguided hands

still i can't imagine
what it would cost
to build a movie monster
like you.

Thistle in the Snake Grass

for kell robertson

somewhere the wind
echoes your song
from when you were
just a boy
whistling into
the past.

Leaving Home or Toledo in October

it finally feels like i've been gone
cold air fills my lungs
like a blackbird
no longer capable of magic
who can stay & die
or simply choose
to fly away.

Poem for Steve Goldberg

there is an entire city
inside your heart

no gloves with holes
in the fingertips
keep it warm
we need you here.

Trailer Park Song, 1984

john cougar mellencamp sings
a song
about peace
in the elementary school cafeteria
as his niece beams with pride

my father fixes a local newscaster's car
in the snow for $5 an hour
to feed a family of four
his knuckle busted open
face covered in blood & grease
like war paint
in a losing battle

in our house
it's difficult
to have any fight left in you
when the spaghetti is low

but peace is not
the same thing
as peace of mind.

Toronto Poem, 1992

we never quite made it there
a flat tire on the canadian side
of the falls

a motel that had the same name
as my favorite aunt
was apparently a sign
from the road trip gods
that we were meant
to eat bad eggs
with glasses
of room temperature pulp
in a cramped cell
that someone had
likely died in.

Poem for Gerard Malanga, 2013

pairs of black chinos
stacked floor to ceiling
can't hold in your ghosts
any better than the memory
of a chasing an italian girl
halfway around the world
nostalgia packed away in a suitcase
with a bullwhip from 1967
the flash of a photograph
like a song
only meant to last
a brief moment.

A Riddle for Sam Ryan in the Afterlife

if you laugh in the woods
& there's nobody there to hear it
does the heartbreak ever go away?

Sam Ryan in the Pandemic

you would've chased love
around the entire city

an irish song
belted out
with your last bit
of breath.

Mythology in the Missouri Woods in Winter

each dog was named
after a greek god here
but the wind
has no respect for time
& once you've pierced the skin
tails just won't wag
like palsied hands
reaching for a water bowl.

Poem for Jim the Bastard, with his Trump Flag Flying

pigs just aren't loyal
they'll eat their own shit
like most of the people
on this street
squealing in the daylight
of the 21st century.

The First Thing Earl Sees in Heaven

for steven miller

a security booth
with a nice firm chair
with plenty of room
to dance.

The Second Thing Earl Sees in Heaven

for brandt dykstra

a pair of buzzers
to trim his hair
by moonlight

as tina turner plays
on a boombox
with his home address
written in magic marker
on the side.

Omaha Song

for larry gawel

brautigan in a free bin
a single torn page
a flag
waving.

Once Around the Cemetery

for my parents in september

we came here
looking for ourselves
younger
thinner
but the birds sing
for someone else
the sun turns into granite
& arrowheads
hidden in the leaves
rustle us from invisible barstools
from cement mixers
from that one girl
who will never die
in our memory
the light bouncing off her sunglasses
flying off the side of a bridge
in irwin pennsylvania
in the winter of 1987
her name written
in spray paint
that will never
fade away
in the rain.

Poem for My Brother, in the Basement

the war of the roses still rages here
in a land of high end weed
& used guitars
the blues are real
the ghost of robert johnson
floating through the suburbs
from the tip
of your hand rolled cigarettes
putting up posters
for lost dogs
in youthful songs of angst

knowing that if anyone
could really see you
they might run you
right out of town.

The Body of An 80 Year Old Man

you think to yourself

i have the body
of an 80 year old man
& the memories too

one day
i'll give them
back.

Trailer Park Song, 1985

two feet of snow
forgotten homework
the night before
hiding behind
a wooden bus shed
like an animal
with its tail
shaking.

Omaha Song #2

for brett jurgens

a quiet leaf never trembles
when looking at its own reflection
taking in everything

i think of you
on windy nights
leaving every stone
left unturned
as a blessing.

Jason Ryberg's Beauty Sleep, in
Carrollton, Missouri

you twist & turn
on a borrowed couch
at some point
we are all
chubby checker's nightmare.

Poem for Vickie & Al, in the Greensburg Terminal, 1995

a quiet cough
sometimes sounded
like the cry
of a dying rooster
on a speeding bus
where half a cigarette
was worth more
than all
of our lives
combined.

Poem Inspired by Ed Smith

inspired
perspired
when i sweat
it's only a fear
of rain.

Poem Inspired by Ed Smith #2

don't touch me
i'm not tired
let's dance
sit the fuck down.

Punk Rock is Cool for the End of the World

for ed smith

you can't hear screaming
over the sound of the radio
on a wooded highway
where a cat curls up
with the noise of youth
forgetting there was ever a time
& place for anger
before just diving into a mosh pit
of rivers & more rivers.

Omaha Song #3

for jay kreimer

one man's swamp
is a field filled with music

an old tire swing
a lonely swimming pool
with grass turned brown

where every girl
is a metaphor
for a firefly
drowning in an
empty
beer bottle.

Poem for Frank Klapak in 1994

i wanted the girls
to look at me
the way they
looked at you

it was such a waste
you never even noticed
your poems about the beatles
were better than the beatles themselves

you had everything

a song without music
a hot cup of coffee
red wine from a dented flask
given to you by an ex-girlfriend in 1968
a torn t-shirt for the british invasion
bought in a used record store in pittsburgh
& girls lining up
to brush the snow
off of the edges
of your coat.

John Dorsey lived for several years in Toledo, Ohio. He is the author of several collections of poetry, including *Teaching the Dead to Sing: The Outlaw's Prayer* (Rose of Sharon Press, 2006), *Sodomy is a City in New Jersey* (American Mettle Books, 2010), *Tombstone Factory,* (Epic Rites Press, 2013), *Appalachian Frankenstein* (GTK Press, 2015) *Being the Fire* (Tangerine Press, 2016) and *Shoot the Messenger* (Red Flag Poetry, 2017), *Your Daughter's Country* (Blue Horse Press, 2019), *Which Way to the River: Selected Poems 2016-2020* (OAC Books, 2020), and *Afterlife Karaoke* (Crisis Chronicles, 2021). His work has been nominated for the Pushcart Prize, Best of the Net, and the Stanley Hanks Memorial Poetry Prize. He was the winner of the 2019 Terri Award given out at the Poetry Rendezvous. He may be reached at archerevans@yahoo.com.